To: Jerry!

Trust God in all things!.
— Terrence

Matthew 28:19
God Bless
Patrice

Be Blessed

In the Moment

Terrence Pope,
Patrice Mozee,
Cheriff Morgan

authorHOUSE®

AuthorHouse™
1663 Liberty Drive, Suite 200
Bloomington, IN 47403
www.authorhouse.com
Phone: 1-800-839-8640

First published by AuthorHouse 4/14/2009

ISBN: 978-1-4389-4412-8 (sc)

Printed in the United States of America
Bloomington, Indiana

This book is printed on acid-free paper.

Pictured on cover: Christian Russell.
Poems and introductions written by Catherine Renee Ross-Cook.
Photos taken by Patrice Mozee, author photo taken by Amy Lugibihl.

Who do we call on in times of trouble? What does God tell us when we suffer pain? When do we turn to God? Where should we go when in doubt?

How does God answer our questions?

This book is about the glory of God and encouraging all who have suffered a loss.

1 Peter 5:10: *"In his kindness God called you to share in his eternal glory by means of Christ Jesus. So after you have suffered a little while, he will restore, support, and strengthen you, and he will place you on a firm foundation.*

There were many young lives taken by violence in the year of 2007, however one young man's life—not his death—touched us in a profound way. His life had an ordained purpose. Ephesians 1:11: *"Furthermore, because we are united with Christ, we have received an inheritance from God, for he chose us in advance, and he makes everything work according to his plan."* From his purpose, we were motivated to share God's word with you. Mark 16:15: *"And he said to them, "Go into all the world and preach the gospel to the whole creation." (RSV)*

Our efforts are dedicated to inspire you to trust in the Lord for everything. Psalm 33:4: *"For the word of the Lord holds true, and we can trust everything He does."* In times of trouble remember Psalm 91: 15: *"When they call on me, I will answer; I will be with them in trouble. I will rescue and honor them."* In times of fear, Isaiah 12:2: *"See, God has come to save me. I will trust in him and not be afraid. The Lord God is my strength and my song, he has given me victory."* In times of doubt, Mark 9:23-24: *"And Jesus said to him, "If you can? All things are possible to those who believe."* Immediately the father of the child cried out and said, "I believe; help my unbelief."*

The answer to all questions and life's circumstances lies within His word. Hebrews 6:18

"So God has given both his promise and his oath. These two things are unchangeable because it is impossible for God to lie. Therefore, we who have fled to him for refuge can have great confidence as we hold to the hope that lies before us. This hope is a strong and trustworthy anchor for our souls. It leads us through the curtain into God's inner sanctuary."

1 Corinthians 2: 9 (NLT)

... "No eye has seen, no ear has heard and no mind has imagined what God has prepared for those who love him."

Dedication

The process of bringing these words of our Living God to you was an exciting and joyous journey. Each time we came together in the Lord we discovered something new about the Word and each other.

We dedicate this effort to our individual earth angels

Dave, Miss Bunny and Maggie

This project started because a child's life was taken due to a senseless act of violence and the child's act of bravery to save another. We are keeping in prayer the families of the Chicago Public School Children who have endured a tragic loss of life and unimaginable pain as a result of violence.

All our Love, during all
Your moments,
Patrice, Terry, & Cheriff

Proverbs 16:24 *(NLT)*

Kind words are like honey sweet to the soul and healthy for the body.

Table of Contents

Introduction

You know it is time to move on, but memory has you bound to pain and suffering. In order to grieve, we must remember the one whom we have loved. There is hope for those whose hearts are empty. Jesus seeks to fill your void. When We Remember is dedicated to shaping your remembrance process. These scriptures will guide you as you commemorate your loved one, while turning to God in your sorrow.

When We Remember

I remember my loved one, oh so close in my arms.

My child, my spouse, my friend
she who would walk with me until the end.
How am I to surrender my love for her?
How am I to release her soul unto eternity
when I know I will cry out for her to the depths
of infinity?

Someone please tell me how do I embrace the
fate of love that now survives only
as an etch in time,
a picture,
a memory?

Catherine Renee Ross-Cook

2 Samuel 1:11-12 *(NIV)*

David and his men tore their clothes in sorrow when they heard the news. They mourned and wept and fasted all day for Saul and his son Jonathan and for the Lord's army and the nation of Israel, because they had died by the sword that day.

These verses tell us that we need not feel insecure or ashamed to openly grieve in our pain. God knows our emotions; and like all that God has to offer these emotions are a gift. David and his men felt sorrow, because in one day they lost their king and David's close friend Jonathan. One should never believe that showing our grief is a sign of weakness. Expressing grief will help purge our intense sorrow when a loved one dies.

2 Samuel 12:22-23 *(NIV)*

He answered, "While the child was still alive, I fasted and wept. I thought, "Who knows? The Lord may be gracious to me and let the child live. But now that he is dead, why should I fast? Can I bring him back again? I will go to him, but he will not return to me."

How can we understand why a child dies? What can be more devastating? The lesson here is trust. Although we cannot fathom the natural purpose, we must trust God's spiritual purpose. King David understood that his son was now with his eternal Father. David prayed while the child was alive; and when God gave his answer, David accepted God's will.

Isaiah 40:11 (NLT)

He will feed his flock like a shepherd. He will carry the lambs in his arms, holding them close to His heart. He will gently lead the mother sheep with their young.

Visualize God as a shepherd, gently tending to and caring for his flock with love. When He takes one of His children to be with Him, He will hold them close. He will guide the ones who are caring for His lambs into a heavenly assurance that her baby is in His care.

Psalm 16:9-11 (NLT)

No wonder my heart is glad, and I rejoice. My body rests in safety. For you will not leave my soul among the dead or allow your holy one to rot in the grave. You will show me the way of life granting me the joy of your presence and the pleasures of living with you forever.

David knew that God can give life even in times of death. When we follow the direction of God, he leads us to an internal joy that will sustain us through whatever troubles we encounter. _

Matthew 5:4 (NIV)

Blessed are those who mourn, for they will be comforted.

Many commentators of the Bible have suggested that the content here of Jesus' teaching, outlines the substance of Christian faith. Jesus begins to teach about self examination and our positional relationship with God. In this verse, God declares from His sovereign position of authority, that those who mourn shall be comforted. In essence, God is calling all believers to "be" in agreement with what He has declared concerning their lives. And if you are in mourning, God in accordance with His word will send you a comforter. The Comforter will be with you and bear with you in your time of need.

Apostle Kevin E. Dean

Genesis 50: 1 (NIV)

Joseph threw himself on his father and wept over him and kissed him.

Joseph truly mourned over the death of Jacob. Expressing to others our feelings of grief when we lose a loved one helps us to recover. We must give ourselves time for the healing process to begin.

Nehemiah 1:4 (NIV)

When I heard these things, I sat down and wept. In fact, for days I mourned, fasted, and prayed to the God in heaven.

In tough situations, it is okay to shed a tear and go through a period of discomfort. Nehemiah demonstrates an example of how to weep, and also, how to get through. He stopped to seek God's attention. Nehemiah fasted to change his focus; and he prayed to hear and receive God's plan. *Christopher Meaders*

Romans 12:15 (NIV)

Rejoice with those who rejoice; mourn with those who mourn.

Introduction

What do you do when the storm does not cease? The tears flow daily, and yet the anguish remains the same. You are drowning in your sorrow; and the words from family and friends provide no lasting comfort. Even If It Rains reminds us that there is a God whose son walked on water. The selected scriptures personify the power God has when light succumbs to darkness, the winds blow, and the rain steadily falls.

Even If It Rains

I shed a tear yesterday Lord.

Was that not enough?

Your word says in time it will get easier,

but yet with each waking moment, this going gets more
and more tough.

You asked me can I stand the rain and I answered
yes.

But what I failed to realize is that this storm was really
a test

and that my lesson was submersed in your word

and if I didn't seek ye first,

without you I have not the power to quench my own
undying thirst.

But yet, I can taste the rainfall that is surrounding
me.

Catherine Renee Ross-Cook

11

Job 16:16-17 (NLT)

My eyes are red with weeping dark shadows circle my eyes. Yet I have done no wrong and my prayer is pure.

Ecclesiastes 3:4 (NIV)

A time to weep and a time to laugh, a time to mourn and a time to dance.

Solomon shows that God has different seasons in life for us to experience. Trials and tribulations will come and seemingly contradict the will of God for our lives. The key is remembering that our temporary problems lend themselves to everlasting solutions, as God's power has overcome the world's pain.

Psalm 6:6 (NIV)

I am worn out from groaning; all night long. I flood my bed with weeping and drenching my coach with my tears.

Like David we can be completely open and honest with God. We are no surprise to Him. All of our circumstances are already known. He gave us all of our emotions. Anger, sadness, joy and kindness are all consequences of humanity. David wore himself out crying for justice against those who would harm him. When we are in despair ask God to give us direction to turn that negative into a positive for the glory of God.

Like the constant pouring of rain drops during a thunderstorm, our tears never seem to stop from the pain felt in the time of loss. We can release it all out to God, like David. Our broken hearts will be repaired by God's fixing hands; for certain he will take the pain away.

Psalm 39:12 (NLT)

Hear my prayer, O Lord; listen to my cries for help. Don't ignore my tears. For I am your guest a traveler passing through as my ancestors were before me.

Psalm 126: 5-6 (NIV)

Those who plant in tears will harvest with shouts of joy. They weep as they go to plant their seed but they sing as they return with the harvest.

We should be reminded of the law of sowing and reaping. Although we may sow tears of sorrow, with God we will one day receive tears of joy. Circumstances, situations, and conditions will turn around through God's inexplicable ability to re-establish. Tears are valuable seeds which will bring an increase in joy. Our tears are at times, our praise to God. We need to be patient while waiting for God's wonderful harvest of joy.

Christopher Meaders

Introduction

Many have coined the phrase, "It's not what you go through, but how you go through it." We can rest assured that God understands the turmoil our hearts experience. The winds are going to blow and the tides, at times, will seem too high. We will find ourselves questioning our faith and asking God, why. *Going Through* speaks to these moments of uncertainty. The selected scriptures cultivate an understanding of pressing through the pain to receive the power.

Going Through

The storm roared
and I laughed in his face
I held up my shield and he was stunned by the grace
that surrounds me, moves through me—for greater is he that
is within me.

But as if he could see those inner fears, those quiet doubts,
and silent tears
the storm laughed, "What faith is this that blows with the
wind,
a doubtful heart, earth cannot mend."

I closed my eyes and then I spoke:
"Earth hath no tools for *heavenly* creation
but only those who read the pages between genesis and
revelation
know that god is a god who sits high and looks low
and understands that man can be tossed to and fro
and in the midst of your rain, sleet, hail, or snow,

I'm gone' praise him anyhow,
For after the storm, the harvest will grow.

So what faith is *this*, I thought you knew
I'm on my way to victory, but right now…
I'm just going through."

Catherine Renee Ross-Cook

John 16:33 (NLT)

"I have told you all this so that you may have peace in me. Here on earth you will have many trails and sorrows. But take heart, because I have overcome the world."

Matthew 14:27 (NIV)

But Jesus immediately said to them: "Take courage! It is I. "Don't be afraid."

In this scripture Peter and the other disciples saw Jesus walking on the water and became terrified. Jesus told them as he tells us not to be afraid. When we become afraid or anxious we must focus on Jesus he is with us. Peter walked on water while his focus was on the power of Jesus. It was not until Peter lost focus that he began to sink. Think on Jesus to maintain your faith and focus.

The storms of life come rushing in, taking us off course, tossing us into disarray. Go to God, for he will guide us through turbulent circumstances. We must totally trust and depend on God to calm our despair, for his awesome power can handle any situation.

Job 1: 20-22 (NLT)

Job stood up and tore his robe in grief. Then he shaved his head and fell to the ground to worship. He said, "I came naked from my mother's womb, and I will be naked when I leave. The Lord gave me what I had, and the Lord has taken it away. Praise the name of the Lord."

Job experienced overpowering anguish; however, he did not lose his faith in God. He displayed his humanity when he gave into his emotions. It is not wrong or unseemly to give in to the feelings that were created by God. Like Job even Jesus succumbed to emotions and wept. Admit to yourself, your family, and your friends the feelings you experience during a loss, disappointment, or heartbreak. God understands that in our humanity, we must express that which burdens the heart and soul.

Job 3: 25-26 (NLT)

What I always feared has happened to me. What I dreaded has come true. I have no peace, no quietness. I have no rest: only trouble comes.

What is your worst nightmare? What would cause you to give up? What do you fear the most? Job lost everything, his children, home, livelihood and his friends and wife were at the door ready to leave too. We sometimes think that just because we love God and he loves us that we will not suffer. If you are in the mist of great sorrow or strife, tests or trouble, remember to concentrate on the God that will see you through not on your circumstance. Nothing should separate us from God's love.

In our darkest moments, finding our way seems so unclear. Through it all we may lose our way and suffer unbearable pain along the journey. God is there with us and for us, when we lean on him. He will guide us back on track, with his marvelous light.

John 16:20 (NIV)

I tell you the truth, you will weep and mourn while the world rejoices. You will grieve, but your grief will turn to joy.

In the preceding verse, Jesus prepares His disciples for what will come: the world would rejoice as the disciples wept. But in just three days the disciples would see Jesus again. When life is challenging, keep your eyes on God and His promises.

In our time of weeping and mourning it may appear that the rest of the world is celebrating. But in due time God will turn our distress into joy, and our pain will beget his blessings for our lives. *Christopher Meaders*

1 Thessalonians 4:13 (NIV)

Brothers, we do not want you to be ignorant about those who fall asleep, or to grieve like the rest of men, who have no hope.

This scripture reassures us that we should not be untaught where death is concerned. We are not to grieve or mourn as if the grave is the end; but be assured that there is life beyond what we see. When Christ returns, all believers--- dead and alive--- will be reunited never to suffer or die again. *Christopher Meaders*

Hebrews 2:10 (NLT)

God, for whom and through whom everything was made, chose to bring many children into glory. And it was only right that he should make Jesus, through his suffering, a perfect leader, fit to bring them into their salvation.

Will we follow the leader? Jesus suffered for us to have everlasting life. In our suffering experiences, we can benefit others going through, by reaching out to them. When we reach out we can change their lives for the better. Letting them know help is on the way through Jesus Christ and they are never alone.

Introduction

In our darkest times we find the greatest yearning for change. We grow tired of yesterday's pain and ever eager for new beginnings. As we hold fast to God's unchanging hand, He will lead us into a new season. His word is the blue print for blessed transformations. It's All about Change personifies the truth that the Father sees beyond our circumstances; and greater works wait around the corner if we are willing to turn.

It's All about Change

A friend said I need a clean heart.

My mama said a renewed spirit.

All I know is I woke up today to *yesterday*

and someone needs to tell me how to fix it.

I heard my grandma say "Fake it till you make it."

So I guess, I'll wear the mask.

But what defines if I make it…that's a question I should probably ask.

My girlfriend gave me a book on how to wait in the *meantime*.

But I don't want to repeat the past

and I'm sick of entertaining a tormented mind/It's time

for me to put the past behind and seek that which can rearrange

Cause the fact of the matter is, *I'm* looking for a change.

And after all the opinions, perspectives, vantage points and positions,

I know now that only Jesus has the power

to write *life altering* prescriptions.

Catherine Renee Ross-Cook

1 Peter 1:6-7 (NLT)

So be truly glad. There is wonderful joy ahead, even though you have to endure many trials for a little while. These trials will show that your faith is genuine. It is being tested as fire tests and purifies gold, though your faith is far more precious than mere gold. So when your faith remains strong through many trails, it will bring you much praise and glory and honor on the day when Jesus Christ is revealed to the whole world.

Psalm 31:9 (NIV)

Be merciful to me, O Lord, for I am in distress; my eyes grow weak with sorrow, my soul and my body with grief.

Asking God for mercy during a time of deep emotional turmoil is an acknowledgement that we recognize our true relationship with Him. We need comfort that only He can provide.

The life of a believer has its ups and downs. When we are hurting it is very easy to turn inward and focus on self. In our lowest valleys the Lord will help us, turn to him for he is always there to carry us through.

Like a roller coaster, our life experiences go up and down. All of a sudden we can drop to valleys filled with despair; even then the Lord is with us. He will pick us up no matter how deep the fall.

Psalm 102: 1-7 (NLT)

Lord hear my prayer! Listen to my plea! Don't turn away from me in my time of distress Bend down and listen and answer me quickly when I call you. For my days disappear like smoke, and my bones burn like red-hot coals. My heart is sick, withered like grass, and I have lost my appetite. Because of my groaning I am reduced to skin and bones. I am like an owl in the desert, like a little owl in a far-off wilderness. I lie awake lonely as a solitary bird on a roof.

Prayer changes things! Lost in despair, our mental and physical disposition can wither to nothing. Talk to God, for he hears our every cry. Healthy changes will occur through the Lord, for he will provide.

The imagery portrayed by the psalmist is intense. The prayer being offered is a confession of an unadulterated feeling of abandonment, a mind-set so extreme that nothing in life matters. He knows our every anxiety, affliction, and anguish. This kind of declaration to God is the beginning of relief; God wants us to lean on him at all times. Crying out to the Lord in our pain is not shameful it is a testament of our trust in Him.

Job 6: 8-9 (NLV)

Oh, that I might have my request, that God would grant my desire. I wish he would crush me. I wish he would reach out and kill me.

Have you ever asked God to just kill you now? How many times in our misery have we begged to be released from our pain? The bible lets us know that we are not the first to ask to be out of our misery. Job wanted to give in, and give up. We sometimes feel the same way. God does not grant these types of request; he has bigger and better plans for us. Trusting God in the good times is admirable; however that same level of trust must be continued in the difficult times also. In order for our faith to become stronger it must be exercised. Through all of our struggles big and small trust God, he is in control and he will take care of us.

Psalm 31:14 (NLT)

But I trust in you, O Lord, I say, "you are my God."

We often put our trust in people, only to be let down. Believing and casting all our cares on the Lord enables us to weather the storms of life.

Revelation 21:4 (NIV)

He will wipe every tear from their eyes. There will be no more death or mourning or crying or pain, for the old order of things has passed away.

It's so good to know, that when this earthly journey comes to an end, a new everlasting life begins with our heavenly father. All the cares of this world will be no more. Believers in God will live in joy and peace forever, eternal life is our great reward.

Introduction

There is no time like the present; how true indeed if our present experiences are ordained by God. Waiting on the Lord begets a glorious manifest destiny. There is no time like that which God has appointed. While we would seek to tell God how and when we would like to walk into the next phase of our lives, we must yield to the authority of His marvelous design. At God's Appointed Time celebrates the journey and the victory in manifesting His will.

At God's Appointed Time

I heard your voice from heaven
and I've never heard it before.
It was an earth shaking experience.
I could feel my soul burning for more.

Your scriptures began to fall from my tongue with ease
and had I attempted to shut my lips
I believe my body would have exploded from the inability to
hold my peace.

I heard your voice from heaven
and I've never heard it before.
It was an earth shaking experience.
I could feel my soul burning for more.

The vision was written on my heart and though I did not expect it,
the power of the Holy Ghost filled me and demons had to respect it!

It was not my will but your will
I would have chosen a quick healing
But your will
I would skipped the pain
But your will
I would have journeyed around, under, or over the rain
But your will be done and not my kingdom
but your kingdom come—into my life seven times seven
for

I heard your voice from heaven
and I've never heard it before.
It was an earth shaking experience.
I could feel my soul burning for more!

The victory was always before me.
The harvest was already mine.
So Satan get thee behind
cause I have prayed, fasted, and waited
 for this is
God's appointed time.

Catherine Renee Ross-Cook

Hebrews 10:23-25 (NLT)

Let us hold tightly without wavering to the hope we affirm, for God can be trusted to keep his promise. Let us think of ways to motivate one another to acts of love and good works. And let us not neglect our meeting together as some people do, but encourage one another, especially now that the day of his return is drawing near.

Romans 5:17 *(NLT)*

For the sin of one man, Adam, caused death to rule over many. But even greater is God's wonderful grace and his gift of righteousness, for all who receive it will live in triumph over sin and death through this one man, Jesus Christ.

It takes one to know one. One man, Adam, set into motion disobedience to God's commands and committed the original sin. All generations from that time have reaped the outcome. One man, Jesus set into motion the chance for all mankind to receive victory. Christ offers us the opportunity to receive life through him.

Like dominoes in a row, the first one falls down causing the rest to follow the same pattern. What Adam sinfully started at the beginning, only Jesus Christ could clean up for all of us in the end. We can claim the victory over death and sin through our belief in Jesus Christ.

1 Corinthians 15:54-57 *(NLT)*

Then, when our dying bodies have been transformed into immortal bodies this Scripture will be fulfilled: "Death is swallowed up in victory. O death, where is your victory? O death where is your sting?" For sin is the sting that results in death, and the law gives sin its power. But thank God! He gives us victory over sin and death through our Lord Jesus Christ.

We will live forever! Death takes on a new meaning; it's not the end to life. Through our risen Christ, life for us becomes eternal. Sin and death may cause us to lie down, but our belief in Jesus Christ allows us to rise up and stand with our heavenly Father forever.

Isaiah 25:8 *(NLT)*

He will swallow up death forever. The Sovereign Lord will wipe away the tears from all faces. He will remove the disgrace of his people from all the earth the Lord has spoken.

We have a blessed assurance when the Lord speaks. The destruction of death happened through Jesus Christ. With no question, we can count on the Lord to be true to his word. In the end, no more crying, no more sorrow, all will be right with the Lord.

2 Corinthians 5:1 *(NLT)*

For we know that when this earthly tent we live in is taken down (that is, when we die and leave this earthly body), we will have a house in heaven, an eternal body, made for us by God himself and not by human hands.

Paul lets us know that our earthly temple will be under new construction when we reach our heavenly home. Our new eternal buildings, created by God will stand flawless in every dimension, forever and ever.

Hosea 13:14 (NIV)

"I will ransom them from the power of the grave. I will redeem them from death. Where, O death are your plagues? Where, O grave is your destruction? I will have no compassion."

Daniel 12:13 *(NLT)*

As for you, go your way until the end. You will rest, and then at the end of the days, you will rise again to receive the inheritance set aside for you.

Daniel refused to bow to the king; he stayed devoted to the word of God for his entire life. Even when Daniel's life was in jeopardy he maintained his trust that God would give him justice. God says he will give us rest and we will receive our heavenly birthright in God's eternal kingdom. Dedication to God has a rich reward.

Isaiah 41:13 *(NLT)*

For I hold you by your right hand, I the Lord your God. And I say to you don't be afraid, people of Israel, for I will help you.

Can you feel his touch? God is holding our hand, we are connected to him. Whatever comes our way, the Lord is there, we cannot lose.

John 8:51 *(NLT)*

I tell you the truth, anyone who obeys my teaching will never die.

What could be simpler, Jesus says those who obey his instructions won't die. Physical death will come, but those who follow Christ will be raised to live forever with him.

Revelation 14:13 (NLT)

And I heard a voice from heaven saying, "Write this down: Blessed are those who die in the Lord from now on. Yes, says the spirit, they are blessed indeed, for they will rest from their hard work; for their good deeds follow them!"

Believers in Christ sow seeds that harvest long after death. Their work to the glory of God has benefits for them and generations to come. Living a lifestyle for Christ produces rewards on earth and in heaven.

Hebrews 3:13-14 (NLT)

You must warn each other every day, while it is still "today," so that none of you will be deceived by sin and hardened against God. For if we are faithful to the end, trusting God just as firmly as when we first believed we will share in all that belongs to Christ.

Talking to other believers every day will help to keep our minds renewed. These shared biblical values help keep us grounded and watchful to the treachery of sin. We must try to maintain the same level of faith that we had when we first became believers. Giving and taking encouragement from each other with love.

John 11:4 (NLT)

But when Jesus heard about it he said, "Lazarus's sickness will not end in death. No, it happened for the glory of God so that the son of God will receive glory from this."

When we face difficulty do we complain and blame God for our circumstance? The truth that believers should always strive to hold fast is that God can turn any bad situation around for His glory. When difficulty comes; as it surely will, first pray for guidance, then see your problem as an opportunity to honor God.

2 Timothy 4:6-8 (NLT)

As for me, my life had already been poured out as offering to God. The time of my death is near. I have fought the good fight, I have finished the race, and I have remained faithful. And now the prize awaits me, the crown of righteousness, which the Lord, the righteous Judge, will give me on the day of his return. And the prize is not just for me but for all who eagerly look forward to his appearing.

Wow! What confidence! Paul faced his death with steadfast assurance that he would see God. He had no fear, no doubt, and was unfazed by what we all will someday face. Paul tells Timothy with certainty that because he lived as God directed him, his blessed reward is waiting for him. We all can have this same resolute belief as Paul, if we just stand firm on His word.

Colossians 1:11 (NLT)

We also pray that you

will be strengthened with

all his glorious power

so you will have all the

endurance and patience

you need. May you be

filled with joy.

Loss, grief can come in many forms: the loss of a loved one, a co-worker, friend, a pet, or the loss of a relationship. I have experienced them all; and although some of the losses were years ago, I find that I have yet to truly recover completely---unable to move past the loss and into the healing process. Work on this project became personal, as I began to recognize that I needed to work, watch and pray to help myself move into the healing process.

As I extend understanding, I also receive understanding, comfort and peace!

To God be the glory.

Cheriff

The loss of a loved one can truly be devastating. When approached to work on this effort, the pain was fresh, because the loss of my Mother had me in the moment. They say, timing is everything and I really didn't know if this was the right time for me to embark on such a journey. Becoming part of the team and in researching God's word to help someone else, who may be going through their moment of grief, helped me to understand and ease my pain. I believe the Lord will always give us what we need, and hopefully this book will aid when you find yourself In The Moment.

Terry

This paragraph was very difficult. I started and stopped more times than I want to remember. It seemed that each time I sat down to put together *just a few words,* I would think about the death of my Father. The thoughts and words would end up as tears, because it still hurts, because I still miss him.

The process of comforting others with the word of God has comforted me. The examination, study and revelation I received with my *friends in faith, has been a joy beyond explanation. Thank you God and Thank you friends!*

Patrice

2 Thessalonians 2: 16-17 (NLT)

Now may our Lord
Jesus Christ himself
and God our father,
who loved us and
by his grace give us
eternal comfort and a
wonderful hope, comfort
you and strengthen
you in every good thing
you do and say.

Acknowledgments

We give honor and praise to God for leading us on this journey.

We also give our deepest thanks to Toni, Derrick, Chris, Kevin, Bob, Catherine, and Jeff.

To Starbucks and Borders, we appreciate the accommodations.

NOTES

NOTES

Printed in the United States
219252BV00002B/5/P